UNDERSTANDING THE WORLD

Edited by

Becki Mee

First published in Great Britain in 1999 by
POETRY NOW
Remus House,
Coltsfoot Drive,
Woodston,
Peterborough, PE2 9JX
Telephone (01733) 898101
Fax (01733) 313524

All Rights Reserved

Copyright Contributors 1999

HB ISBN 0 75430 656 9
SB ISBN 0 75430 657 7

FOREWORD

Although we are a nation of poets we are accused of not reading poetry, or buying poetry books. After many years of listening to the incessant gripes of poetry publishers, I can only assume that the books they publish, in general, are books that most people do not want to read.

Poetry should not be obscure, introverted, and as cryptic as a crossword puzzle: it is the poet's duty to reach out and embrace the world.

The world owes the poet nothing and we should not be expected to dig and delve into a rambling discourse searching for some inner meaning.

The reason we write poetry (and almost all of us do) is because we want to communicate: an ideal; an idea; or a specific feeling. Poetry is as essential in communication, as a letter; a radio; a telephone, and the main criteria for selecting the poems in this anthology is very simple: they communicate.

CONTENTS

Title	Author	Page
Rejoice	David A Bray	1
Moving House	N C Bain	2
My Friends	Helen Gill	3
A Secret Place	Pam Gibbons	4
Do You Believe	S Barjona	5
Grandad's Return	Pauline Madden	6
Environment	Erika Duncan	8
Bare Facts	Jan Andersen	9
The Childhood Campaign	Jackie Makepeace	10
The Weekend Call	Maria Bernadette Potter	11
Our Little Ones	Patricia Lynwood	12
The Special Words Of A Child	Peter Comaish	13
Mosquito	G E Mills	14
The Euro	Peter Hicks	15
Snapshot	H Lincoln	16
We've Spent It	Philip Trivett	17
The Marching Peacocks	Geraldine Bruce	18
Avigor Goldsmith Stain Glass	J Dunkley	19
On Standby	Rachel Evans	20
Awakening	Danielle Gallagher	21
What Is A Day?	Jasmine Dienes-Stevens	22
The First	Steven Gill	23
Sweet Dreams	Carolyn Long	24
PMT	Jonathan Covington	26
Millennium Moan	Josephine Gill	27
Millennium Bug	Simon Baxter	28
Gun, With Silencer Attached	Anthony Lascelle	29
Going Beggin	David Hulme	30
Winter Came Upon A Summer Day	Glyn Davies	31
Submersion	Timothy C Jefferies	32
A Bird's Eye View Of Britain	J F Jenkins	33
Mind Paralysis	John Robertson Veir	34
Learn To Complain	Angela Pritchard	35
Just The Blues	Katherine Carter	36

A Slight Return	E D Jones	37
The Gods Of Flesh	Carl Anthony Dignan	38
Crabs	Mark Baker	39
Parental Choice	S Mullinger	40
The Third Millennium	William Edward M Phillips	41
No Time To Stop	G M Cooper	42
Believe It	L Hammond/Oberansky	43
Oliver Twist And The Poetaster	Les Merton	44
Puddled!	Christopher Higgins	46
The 'Option' Of No	Mildred F Barney	47
Let Loose	James Reid	48
Mathematics	Sharon Clarke	49
The Computer	Moira H Thorburn	50
Time Of Change	J P Smyth	51
Battered, Scattered - Going There	Tom Scott	52
Ultimathe Ulae	Mandy Holten	54
Natives	Fiona Higgins	55
I Give You Science	Joan E Blissett	56
Specks Of Dust	Jean Oxley	57
Millennium Vacancy	Roman Suchyj	58
My Hope	Joan Picton	59
Careless!	Benny Howell	60
As To Smiling At Work	Robert Denis Spencer	61
Freedom Of Choice	Henry J Green	62
Workhorse	Barbara Dudley	64
Poets Of Today	Alma Montgomery Frank	65
Hmmm . . . Well!	Mike Bradley	66
The Unfortunate	Steven Jenkins	67
Street Code	Trevor Hussey	68
You?	Angel Blue	69
Sensitive Siren	Lesley Lewis	70
Standing On The Edge Of The World	Coral Spark	71
There's No Joy On Those Streets	Leslie Fine	72
The Enemy Within	Alexis Stearns	74
Facade	Caroline J Sammout	75

Night Thoughts	Betty Harness	76
The Best Of British	Heather D Hill	77
The Best Of British	Audrey Allen	78
The Night Raid	Richard Reeve	79
The Best Of British	Beryl Moorehead	80
Best Of British	Ruth Wright	81
Best Of British	Jeanne Ison	82
Made In Britain	P R Canham	84
Made In England	Charles Green	85
In My Day	Florence Davies	86
Victim TV	Sean Brown	87
Today's World	Doris I Livesey	88
Justice For Stephen Lawrence	Saheeda Khan	89
Mask	Liana Cougar	90
Apocalypse	Ann Hathaway	91
Victoria Falls	Lee Round	92
Hopes And Dreams	Joan Heybourn	93
A Single Mother's Dream	B Marshall	94
Moving	Andrea Kenkmann	95
Come With Me, Love	Michael Pendragon	96
Resurrection	Tom Ritchie	97
An Age-Old Abortion	August Head	98
Dysfunction Junction	Aron M Smith	100
Time Being	D A Warren	102
My Lover And Me	Helen Jane Bailey	103
Falling Apart	T Burke	104
The Lawyer - Mrs Rosemary Nelson	Kim Montia	105
Confidence	Anne Beard	106
Confusion	Gillian Weaving	107
Hands Off Our Pound	Rosa Riley	108
A Friend Concerned	Saheeda Khan	109
She	Chantelle Patterson	110
The Yuppy	Colin Allsop	111
The Twenty-First Century	D S M	112
Last Ring Call For Slapstick Clowns	Gillian C Fisher	113
Best Of British	Trudi Webber	114

Best Of British	Winifred Lund	115
The Cause	Arthur Denny	116
Earth Man	Jean Paisley	117
How To Create A Rose	Teresa Connolly	118
The Millennium Year	Frank Scott	119
A Pensive Ride	Margaret Gleeson Spanos	120
To Myself	Anna Virkerman	121
Opening	Hannah Shooter	122

REJOICE

Rejoice in the name of Jesus
And how he died for thee
Rejoice in the name of Jesus
In fear of Calvary rejoice in
The name of Jesus and all
The love he brings rejoice
In the name of Jesus our Saviour
Friend and our King.

David A Bray

MOVING HOUSE

Today's the day we are to move from our house of twenty years
take with us all our goods including those faithful rusty garden shears
packing cases full to the brim and furniture stacked on high
removal men grunt and groan, their efforts their physiques belie.

Soon the house stands empty and still and echoes to the sound of the
                                                                                                  wind
a feeling of quiet hurt descends as if against the house we've sinned
memories flood back suddenly of times and dramas we had there
to the house we were its life, our souls in it we laid out bare.

The kids have known no other house, our trusty fortress on the estate
soon we will live in a newly-built one with a small garden and a brand
                                                                                                 new gate
We sigh and look back as we depart, fondness in our voices so clear
our old house we regarded as a friend and we truly loved the bricked
                                                                                                 old dear.

N C Bain

My Friends

Horses - horses
Some black - some white.
Alert - watchful
All day - sometimes night
Living together
In all weather.

Horses - horses
Some big - some small
Dappled colours
The best of all.
Each one lovely
Gentle creatures -
Loyalty perhaps
Best of features.

Look in their eyes
And you will find
Faithfulness - love
Of special kind
A trustfulness
Which makes you proud
They've picked you out
From all the crowd -
      My lovely friends.

Helen Gill (13)

A Secret Place

There is a secret place within my heart
Where memories of love will never part.
My childhood was protected, wrapped in care
Thanks to my grandmother who was always there.

Youth should have been carefree and gay
But war came, young men went away.
In spite of this we had our share of fun
And made the most of life 'til peace was won.

Twenty-one, I wedded a fine man
And married life with all its joys began.
Two children, first a girl and then a boy
Came to crown my pinnacle of joy.

Hard times were had but then that's life:
How can we learn to care not knowing strife?
Give freely help to those who suffer
And render hope - a future proffer!

So now you see my heart's full store
Where reminiscences abide galore.
Five grandchildren delight me now, such dears,
What better life could fill my latter years.

Pam Gibbons

DO YOU BELIEVE?

Do you believe in fairy tales?
I didn't till I met you.
Do you believe in wishing wells?
I didn't till I met you.
Do you believe as lovers do,
fall in love at first sight?
I didn't till I met you.

Do you believe when people say,
That love will never last?
I did till I met you.
Did you believe that I'd fall in love?
I did when I met you.
Now I believe in all these things,
Do you?

S Barjona

GRANDAD'S RETURN

Grandad, was a real delight
Michael loved him with all his might
But on one real sad, sad day
Grandad got sick and passed away
Michael, being only three years old
Had no comprehension of what he'd been told
He couldn't really understand
Why his lovely Grandee was no longer around

After many weeks had passed
Mike and mum were all aghast
When on one cold and wintry night
The shilling went in the electric light
The two were all alone in the dark
Even the dog was afraid to bark
Mum was scared as scared could be
She took her son upon her knee
She said 'Oh Mike, let's go to bed!'
Up the stairs with him she fled

Mum tucked up Michael safe and sound
And stood and had a look around
There was not a lot that she could see
It was dark as dark as dark could be
All of a sudden from out of the dark
Came Michael's small voice 'Look Mummy, look'
'What is it Mike' she said with fright
'Oh look Mummy' he said with sheer delight
'Grandee has come to see us tonight'
'What are you saying Mike?' she said
Trying hard to see her small son in the bed
'You know your Grandad is now in heaven'
But Michael insisted, he was here in our haven

Mum's hair stood on end. She thought she would choke
Her tongue rolled to the back of her throat
'Behind you Mum, just have a look'
'No chance' she said 'I've had enough'
Half undressed she grabbed her son, down the stairs with him she run
Mum ran down the stairs two at a time and through the front door
in double quick time.

Out on the street on this cold wintry night
The front door slammed with all of its might
Has there ever been anyone had such a fright?
Mum came to her senses and cuddled her son
Who looked puzzled whilst sucking his thumb
Now she was back to stark reality
Both were stranded without a key
She stood on the doorstep still shaking and crying
Trying desperately to put a brave face on.

'So Grandad we all love you
We miss you terribly
But if you come to see us
Don't show yourself to me'

Pauline Madden

ENVIRONMENT

E very animal should live in a clean and safe environment
N ever drop rubbish
V ehicles waste our earth
I s war necessary?
R oads are always being built
O ur planet needs our help
N ow is the time to act
M otorbikes don't make as much pollution as cars
E veryone and everything has a right to live
N uclear warheads are not needed
T he environment is our home and we should respect it.

Erika Duncan (11)

BARE FACTS

'Why's *that* man got no hair?'
Asked Edward in an embarrassingly loud voice.
That man overheard and smiling at the young boy said,
'Alas, I have no choice.
When I was your age I had lots of hair,
With lustrous blond curls galore,
But then my hair stopped growing, whilst my head carried on,
So it doesn't fit anymore.'

Jan Andersen

THE CHILDHOOD CAMPAIGN

My first born was suddenly old enough to start
Pre-school aged 3. Three. When did that happen?
It seems only moments ago, through battle-cries and
bruises, that I released him into this world and cradled
him for hours and hours like a hostage; security for my
own fulfilment. Trepidation's triggered a declaration
that no harm would come to him and I prepared myself
to defy any evil, harmful device which may stumble into
his path. A fully enrolled combatant. He relied completely
on my every move, which in a way, comforted me. Unaware
that I was giving him his own independence, he started doing
things for himself, rendering me redundant from my rank.
I started to panic. He's growing up and forming a
mind of his own. What if he doesn't need me as much and
maybe one day, turns against me, forgetting his alliance?

And while all these thoughts were firing through my
mind as I picked him up from school, he looked
right into my eyes and said, without any prompting
or encouragement, calming all my concerns 'Mummy
I happy.'

The war with my fears was over.

Jackie Makepeace

THE WEEKEND CALL

In the morning, of a weekend,
Quality time we'd often spend
Woken with soft puckered lips,
You feel their tiny fingertips.

Their light warm bodies jump up close,
Love better than a tonic dose.
Kiss and hold their bodies little,
Then enjoy a game of tickle.

Count their fingers, count their toes.
Brush their hair and stroke their nose.
Singing songs and telling rhymes.
Remember these are special times.

Maria Bernadette Potter

OUR LITTLE ONES

Every bright eye
        and each pretty cheek,
                young vibrant life
                        a demeanour so meek,
can change in a instant
to temper and screams,
if purpose is thwarted
and new freedom gleams.

        They inspire as they blossom
                yet can drive us insane,
                        exhausting and delightful,
                                but who'd have them change.

They stretch and extend us
'til we nearly break,
mature us, and take from us
so much that is fake.

Now it's time to admit
        how special young ones are,
                not only human children
                        but Earth creatures near and far.

        They're our investment in the future,
        our belief in the past,
        life precious in the present
        is what our young ones ask.

Patricia Lynwood

THE SPECIAL WORDS OF A CHILD

It's not because
they're always right
or full of fun
or simply bright
but well behind
each cheeky smile
I know what's meant
exactly!

Peter Comaish

Mosquito

Made of wood, in a metal age
Light and strong beyond compare
Sleek of line, with ample speed
Made her queen of all the air

From Freeman's folly, to Wooden wonder
Her strength was really in her skin
She had no need of criss-cross frames
This streamline shape, with classy fin.

Her speed and grace outshone the rest
On high, at range or dashing low
Unarmed she bombed, or as fighter served
From wartime sky striking blow on blow.

On recce flights, she mapped from high
Or targets marked through shot and shell
Smashed trains and roads till nothing moved
Bombed prison walls, until they fell.

A throaty roar, from Merlins came
The fleeting shape 'twixt branch and leaf
The blast of cannon and browning chatter
As dashing low, she bared her teeth.

Gone the days of bitter struggle
Freedom's air which cost us dear
She was the one they fought and flew then
A friend so good, a foe to fear.

Dashing roaring into history
She smashed from high the Nazi foe
Her crews were daring, their lifeblood giving
Men breathed her name, 'Mos-quit-o'!

G E Mills

THE EURO

We've heard about the Euro and now it's on the scene,
It could lead us to disasters such as there have never been.
Politicians and big business say that we're being left behind,
But people of this nature have all an axe to grind.
Politicians have in Europe an enormous gravy train,
Whilst multinationals' profits will definitely gain.
I still do not believe their line, convince me if you can,
That there'll be advantage in it for the normal working man.

It's not just economics, as they tell us day by day,
But controlling politicians, so we can have our say.
there's some control of Westminster, but for heaven's sake,
Commissioners and MEPs are clearly on the make.
They churn out documents and rules, pouring out their faxes,
It simply means that all of us will be paying higher taxes.
Our government will lose its power and to be truly frank,
There's no single democratic thread in the European bank.
In the European elections now, the voting's not the same,
We'll be casting votes for parties, for candidates with no name.

So I say to politicians, who want to jump the gun,
Just hang back a moment, let's walk before we run.
Don't tell us what will happen, it's inevitable we join,
It's absolutely crucial that we take the Euro coin.

We need a referendum now, so that we can all tell you,
What the bulk of the electorate consider you should do.
We were brought up British, that's the way we'd like to stay,
God help the politicians who throw democracy away!

Peter Hicks

SNAPSHOT

A perfect photo, licence or passport,
With a white background preferably sought
To suit yourself, is easy to obtain.
First adjust the seat height near the frame,
Hold both knees to left or right. Turn your head
And shoulders. Then relax and look again.
With chin held high lean back instead
To flatter and identify the name.

H Lincoln

WE'VE SPENT IT!

If God's grace could be earnt,
would we be in this state?
When we look, fear and tremble
at the beef on our plate
and ask 'Is it British?
If so, lunch can wait.'

Would Wesley have thought
that his work may have earned
an extra chance for our nation,
for at least one more century's turn
after the German Army, twice, our land tried to burn?

Did Will Booth ever think
that his work would still be in need?
That the poor, from violence, rape and enslavery
still need to be freed?
That those terrible stains
would still exist and be the same?

I guess we are lucky
that grace demands no pay in return.
For all of those good gifts our nation would earn;
would have all vanished along with our national pride
that once the whole world envied and desired.
For it's only the Nazis who are proud to be British, it seems.
And our Christian heritage is all spent on daydreams!

Philip Trivett

THE MARCHING PEACOCKS

The small girl tried to sleep but tossed, afraid.
The tall dark room, the shadowy night-light
flickering, the warm air wafted upwards -
and still the marching peacocks staved off sleep.

Now across the crescent bay of windows
draped the new curtains, rich brocade monsters
whose patterned peacocks strut in formal grounds
with hollyhocks. And now the deep folds swayed . . .

Was a draught stirring those heavy curtains -
or were the marching peacocks waiting there?

Geraldine Bruce

Avigor Goldsmith Stain Glass

Frantically suffocating
drowning into unconsciousness
sensing only my stiffness
cold chills stirring me
stretching, I struggle
to revive my aching limbs
the cold holds me down
how cruel it is
unable to move, shuddering as
waves continue to lash over me
my eyes seeing golds, greens, reds and blues as
the pain is worse
more seaweeds whip my frozen body
my eyes stir once more
only to see yellow fish
with big black eyes
how can this world of mystic and
colour let me die?

J Dunkley

ON STANDBY

Crushed. She finds herself shackled,
Perpetually, to soured memories.
Stark realisation; everything she believed in -
Gone - like Him.
Hopes fracture. Shattered dreams.
The sweet agony of rejection
Cloaks her; completely enfolding.
Strange comfort in such subversive pain.
Automatic routines remind her
Of all the special moments with Him -
They hardly seem special now.
She becomes insular. Lives in a vacuous world
Full of unfulfillment.
Waiting, waiting, waiting, waiting . . .
. . . For life to happen.
Staring blankly at the screen -
A window to a world where life happens . . .
. . . To other people.
A window of stained glass - shows
The nameless millions who seem to belong -
Shows life happening . . .
. . . To other people.
In the turmoil of today and every day,
She is forgotten, alone, faceless.
She waits and waits her life away
Until what she has waited for . . .
. . . Is forgotten.

Rachel Evans

AWAKENING

From a silent sleep
I can hear the phone,
That everlasting tone,
Up I rise, bleary eyes,
I answer it but there
Is no voice down the line,
There is just silence,
This brings back bad memories,
Who is it? I ask,
Why are you doing this?
My heart starts pondering,
My body aglow,
I am very frightened but
Can't let it show,
It was a malicious phone call,
One of many, you know.

Danielle Gallagher

WHAT IS A DAY?

There is no day
It's just a trick
To make us stay
What *is* a day, anyway?
Condensing Time?
As be as it may
A day is not
The way to play
This planet says
It's rules they lay
We all must pay
Be restricted into
One small day,
Day, then day again
Do you give a jot?
Is this the way?
For dreams,
For play?
The rigid rules
Fixed like solid hay,
Substanceless
Yet seeming strong
No way!
That invention
A Day
Made to merge
Us into Time
A Day *is not*
Unless *you* say
No Day. *No* prior Day:
Only *your* invented Day
Or *non* Day
Equals future play

Jasmine Dienes-Stevens

THE FIRST

A heavy golf bag,
still attached to a price tag.
A brand new ball,
standing proud and tall.

The first tee looms,
a good tee shot or you could face doom,
A flying swing,
then a quiet ping.

A long powerful drive,
finishes with a long curving dive.
The fairway grass is short and green,
but the bunkers look very mean.

A poor fairway shot,
leaves the man blustery and hot.
It still lands on the green,
but leaves a putt in the teens.

The pressure is high and tense,
he marks the ball with a one pence.
The ball rolls dead straight towards the hole,
Yes, it's in like a great goal.

Steven Gill

SWEET DREAMS

He slept along the path
Of those blue darts of Cupid's,
Brought to life
When the whitest wand was waved,
And though the Glories of the Morn
Fell on his face,
The Yellow Broom
Of the black-eyed Nymph of Paradise,
Softly swept them from his face -
She was on guard.
This sweet and scented beauty
Was his prize,
Her smell of Musk and Incense
Puzzled him,
But gentle flowing stream,
Enticed a deeper rest,
He did not know
He was the faithful one,
Rewarded with immortal company.
He dreamt his lips were touched
By honey-dew,
On golden apples
Of the nymph's best crop,
Plucked from a dragon-guarded
Island of the sea
Far to the west
At some uncertain point.
Should he be really blamed
Submitting to the sweetest sleep
That makes him want to stay
In quiet repose.

If eyes are not,
His heart is still awake,
And in his mind,
Her face is clearer still;
Prisms of crystal ice
Made rings around her head,
She beckoned him
To come and take her hand,
Just as he reached
To touch those fragile tips,
Damn!
He woke.
Damn!

Carolyn Long

PMT

What's that got to do with me?
Why, what have I done?
She's arguing again
at the drop of a hat
my oh my nothing ever pleases her
she's at it hammer and tongs
why, what did I do wrong?
Pick, pick, pick, bitch, bitch, bitch
again and again
what have I done to deserve this?
She can be a right old bitch
I put it all down to the five-year itch
when I put on her finger that band of gold
that was the end of all my problems or so I was told!
She's getting right craggy so I'll put it down to age
then again she's only thirty-two
so what's guy supposed to do?
Do I carry on or do I leave?
As you can see I'm really rather peeved
she's got the better of me I'm seeing red
she's sending me off my head
I'm beginning to wish that she was dead
she's on the rag
I'm dying to calm my nerves with a fag
she's got PMT a guy can tell
I'll have to put up with this
after three or four days it's back to wedded bliss

Jonathan Covington

MILLENNIUM MOAN

World, I don't like you anymore. I abhor your de-gen-er-ation.
In dimmed, unstately, strobe-lit pleasure domes,
fixing on the doped lotus blooms of ecstasy,
indecorous, ignoble savages gyrate at Aaron's everlasting party
and senses high, hate sense, not free but slaves
to the madding crowds' unmusical boom tunes,
while glitzy, multimedia stars who sing badly or kick balls,
make their easy millions from poorer multitudes
who worship at their false ephemeral, clay shrines.
They shine more darkly in my different heaven.

World, I don't know you anymore. I deplore your de-val-u-ation
of my sacred values. Your crooked hole-in-the-wall,
current currency dispenser cockily spits out
of its tainted, toothless mouth my credo card,
which expired long since and is now consigned
to past 'unenlightened' decades of ignorance;
and slick superior sandal and anorak loathers
preferring their multiple choice, swifter, surface solutions
look down from jerry-built sandcastle heights on those
who still read books seriously in beautiful ivory towers.

World, I don't need you anymore. I ignore your man-ip-u-lation
of naive, media-mesmerised masses amassing
no original thoughts but brainwashed into crass conformity.
'Get a life!' they sneer, with ugly,
rude, unloving belligerence born of learnt
self-love and hate-asserting unconcern.
'Call that life?' I cry. If that is life
then let me till the day I shuffle
off this godless mortal coil bear witness
to the real life in Christ that never dies.

Josephine Gill

MILLENNIUM BUG

Do you know 'bout the Millennium Bug?
Millennium what? I give a shrug
To be honest I just don't know what you mean
Something next year'll create a scene?
Date and time, time and date
Next year may be just too late?
This computerised insect means nought to myself
Twenty years I've been left on the shelf
Gathering dust, and mental decay
'Millennium Bug' is that what you say?
Since this strange bug's introduction
I've suffered from a subconscious seduction
Who will save me from this millennium creature
Eaten alive by this human flesh-eater?
Spray the land, burn down the crops
Eradicate this beast, pull out all the stops
I'm scared to death, and just don't understand
This marching monster may devour our land
Please, oh please could someone explain
This mental torment may be in vain
But I don't know just what to think
Quickly, pour another drink
The more, the sooner will come the haze
Blank out what the paper says
Help me someone, I'm all alone
No wrong have I ever done
Who will help me during the night
And be my saviour from this fearful plight?
Millennium what? I give a shrug
I know nothing of this Millennium Bug.

Simon Baxter

GUN, WITH SILENCER ATTACHED

mortgage your life
to a faceless world

take from the worthless
endless well,
pay with your soul,

hold out your arms
offer your wrists
for that manufactured
bracelet,

know not of knowledge
only your place,

figure the daily puzzle
on your coffee break,

burn off your calories
and eat well,
cut down on your drinking
stub out your cigarette,

longevity
longevity is what
you need,

the longer you live
the longer you'll
serve.

Anthony Lascelle

GOING BEGGING

This pavement is hard
Bone upon stone
But nothing's as hard as my stare
At the tight-fisted twat
In the black bowler hat
And the neat little parting of hair.

In your camel's hair coat
And the tiniest gloat
You stride by my kerb-level lair
And you glance at my hat
And my bits and my tat
With never a penny to spare.

Go home to your wife
And your desperate half-life
And the comforts you allegedly share
The poison-faced rat
In the black bowler hat
To yours I'll never be heir

And thank God for that
You tight-fisted twat
For I'm rich with the scent of night air
On my throne of a mat
With my this and my that
And the heat from my lingering glare.

David Hulme

WINTER CAME UPON A SUMMER DAY

The warm June sun, in the late afternoon sky.
The smell of the freshly painted park bench,
Mingling, with that of the new-mown grass,
The sound of the now, distant, cutter,
Moaning in unison, with the laughing chatter,
of gleeful, homeward-bound, schoolchildren.
Elder citizens, straw-hatted and floral dressed,
sipping their afternoon teas, beneath parasols.
An idyllic summer scene, some might say,
Yet, bleak mid-winter came upon me,
on that lovely summer's afternoon.
Its icy fingers, gripped my grieving heart,
Its melting snows, drenched my dampened spirit,
Its burning frost, seared my tortured soul
And I knew then, upon that lovely day,
That others, not lesser, but different than I,
had found life far too hard to bear,
When winter came upon them on some summer day.

Glyn Davies

SUBMERSION

Beneath the liquid seams
The stillness of my dreams
Awaits my life's insertion
For severance by submersion

And so I choose to pass
Into a denser mass
For we have made intense
Less denser elements,

And through the looking glass
(My tempered diver's mask)
My jaded eyes behold
Dancing shafts of gold

Whilst fluid wholly holds
My load, supports, enfolds
In balance all my weight -
The pressures of my state,

And so the water's calm
Embalms my mind's alarm,
And there amidst the deep
My cares, awhile, can sleep.

Timothy C Jefferies

A Bird's Eye View Of Britain

Some memories of old England
Made me wince.

Royalty held its grandeur
While many of the poor people
Suffered.

Not that I am jealous of
Wealth. Today I read the
Papers with rapt fascination.
There's so many scandals going
On in high places.

Nowadays the news is made
Much fuller due to the miracle
Of TV satellite.

My boyhood links made me love
The country landscape of the
Cotswolds.

It seems the years have fled.
At 72 when I look in the mirror
I see the face of an elderly
Garden gnome!

Time is of the essence.
Now I live each day to the
Fullest. My battling days are
Over.
What tomorrow brings I accept
Fortune or misfortune and just
Soldier on, to the end.

J F Jenkins

MIND PARALYSIS

Living in a world where you're the contradiction
rational thoughts go out your head.
Everything that's outside is a seduction
panic attack before you're out of bed.
Jigsaw mind at an early hour
another day to face,
an everlasting thought shower
as I stare into space.
Another day of non-production
rational thoughts come in my head,
tomorrow is such a seduction
tranquillised mind in my bed.

John Robertson Veir

LEARN TO COMPLAIN

I was here first!
We hear you say.
Don't push in,
Don't get in my way.

Don't talk like that.
Stand in a queue?
Done it years,
You don't have a clue.

This cup's dirty,
Don't like this tea.
Want more cake,
Don't grumble at me.

It's taken years,
Perfect at last.
Come on dear,
You'd better learn fast.

Angela Pritchard

JUST THE BLUES

Why? On days like this
When you're feeling quite confused
Your life that was once bliss
But now it's just the blues

If you wake up each day
And you're feeling really low
Scared of what to say
'Cos you're ready to explode

Is it like a burning pain
When you're hurt and feel alone
Are you scared it'll be the same
Do you dread going home?

Do you try and try and try
To hold your life together
Or do you breakdown and cry
Will you feel like this forever?

So come on now
It's up to you
It's not for real
It's just the blues.

Katherine Carter

A Slight Return

Well! I stand up next to a watchtower
'Déjà vu' flowing through my mind
You always had this strange effect on me
But I think that you will find,
Even though I haven't heard from you
In such a hell of a long time
The song remains the same, as it always did
I haven't had a change of heart or a change of mind.

Now! From where I'm 'coming from' these days
'Unconventional' is the name of the game
I've had my fill of the 'sheep mentality'
Don't you know it's driving me insane,
I find 'apathy' so hard to deal with
It's time to strike out, and strike out with force
Just got to show a little self-restraint
Just for appearances sake, of course!

Well! Empires rise and empires fall
But it doesn't matter that much to me
I've been reconstructing my internal organisation
Although it's not that obvious to see,
Haven't got any specific targets right now
I've had to leave them all behind
Sometimes you've got to sacrifice things in the short-term
To secure a long-term 'peace of mind'!

E D Jones

THE GODS OF FLESH

Life's no fun when you're in pain
The lust for death drives you insane,
You feel so bad you're dead inside
It hurts so much to stay alive.

The doctors say they do their best
It's all for your own good,
With sympathetic torture
For a life misunderstood.

So we must go on suffering
So they can pay the rent,
How many souls will they bleed dry
Before they will repent?

They must reform their attitude
And try to understand,
The simple right to dignity
Of life held in their hands.

Carl Anthony Dignan

CRABS

Do not rush the wide-backed crabs,
In coats of blue, and greys.
With headscarves and speckled grins,
They'll mount the stairs sideways.

Do not help them with their bags,
That rustle by their sides.
Do not enquire at their caves
And do not look inside.

Wide-backed crabs have served their term,
Sung ordinary songs.
It's time to extinguish them,
Ensuring that they've gone.

Or you'll end up as wide as them
Surrounded by dead eyes.
You'll plod to every order
And never be surprised.

Mark Baker

Parental Choice

I wonder, if I am the only one who doesn't think it right,
All children want the best conditions to learn how to read and write.
To close most selective schools, when for them, there is clearly a need,
As a parent, seems a strange decision, I won't be deceived.
I want children to have a chance, do as well as they are able,
Glad, I live in this area, where a choice of schools is on the table.
Because I should be horrified to find I had no choice at all,
Then, I would soon be out canvassing at my own local town hall.
Seems to me, that politicians who've gained from their selective posts,
Are the people, who want to scrap this kind of education most.
And now could be the time for a new grammar school referendum,
Should more be reopened, listening to ideas of dads and mums.

S Mullinger

THE THIRD MILLENNIUM

Such rain such roaring wind and raging seas,
Foul vapours curling from beneath the clod,
Such chaos quickens evolution's streams
In the Millennium when men ape God.

When all men's dreams have hopelessly gone wrong,
Laid waste the planet and their lives as well,
The meaner species versatile and strong
Contort what could be heaven into hell,

Where alien creatures pick among the bones
And raise antennae to the copper skies.
Brains? God? Whatever worth do these have now?
Remorse? Compassion? Only the wild wind sighs.

William Edward M Phillips

No Time To Stop

Rush, rush here, rush, rush there
no time to stop, no time to care
Rush to work, rush back again
Rush to the shops, rush to the gym
go for your life, no time to be slim

Rush back home, get the fast food cooking
is there time to sit, go on no one's looking

Like tiny ants we hurry about
not going anywhere, jut dashing in and out
How pointless is this, do we really need to be
all victims of stress, where's the harmony?

For once I shall sit in my fireside chair
and ponder my day with a tired-out glare
shall I rush tomorrow there is no doubt
it gives me a reason to scream and shout

I've a thousand pointless things to do
yes I know, don't tell me
so have you

G M Cooper

BELIEVE IT

I longed to live amongst the fields and lanes,
Knit into rural country life, I decided,
This now were for me, the time were ripe;
The quiet tranquil country - where?

Believe me, forget the country, if you care,
For I have never become so aware,
Of the suffering that is there,

The trees blown gentle leaves, the maize
Drifts on a breeze, as sea ebbing back and forth
And all the seasons course,
But for all this, the horrors are worse.

The life of a screaming piglet, taken,
The life of the fox, chased to death,
The charging of shovels and dog's shrill bark as badgers are
                                                      baited, to kill.
Poultry, crammed into steamy humid,
Factory rooms, when usefulness is over, broken necks, their doom.
More tired, than ever, I stand, for I am, in a continual fight,
I care and cannot shut them from sight.
Such injustices, it seems will ever be.

The countryside is not, I now see,
What I thought it would be.
Where I am, I now must stand,
To give my life; with love, help guard from savage hand.

L Hammond/Oberansky

OLIVER TWIST AND THE POETASTER

'To play for Manchester United.'
Frank remembered answering,
his headmaster's ambition question.
'You've got about as much chance
of playing for Manchester United,
as Oliver Twist had of seconds
when he stupidly asked for more.
You should read Oliver Twist boy.'
Was the headmaster's dismissing advice.

Frank never played for Manchester United,
he went to work for the local Co-op.
Frank had a new ambition, to be a poet.
For an unbiased opinion on his first poem,
Frank went to see his old headmaster.

The headmaster read the poem and sighed,
'Did you read Oliver Twist?' he asked.
Frank was prepared for the question,
'I've read Oliver Twist, saw the film
with Alec Guinness as Fagin, the TV
adaptation, plus the musical Oliver,
I know what Oliver Reed as Bill Sykes
wanted to say to Nancy when she asked,
if he loved her, and I've also tasted
the soup Oliver wanted more of.'

'Obviously you know all about Oliver Twist.'
Replied the headmaster, 'I'm sure you will
understand when I say, Oliver would never
have succeeded as a pickpocket, or criminal
no matter how much Fagin wanted him to.'

The headmaster saw Frank to the door,
'The history of the Co-operative Movement
by Agnes Allen is worth reading Frank.'
Was the headmaster's dismissing advice.

Les Merton

PUDDLED!

My bewildered, higgledy-piggledy, confused and puddled brain,
and the rest of my befuddled self is really just the same,
mixed-up and topsy-turvy that's what I am, can't you guess?
How did I get here? How do I get out again from this mess?
How on earth did I get here? Also, where did I come from?
Which way is up? Which way do I go? Oh me, the perplexed one,
with a mouth, a jumbo jet could do a three-point turn in,
and a brain that can be wrapped in a postage stamp, enfolding,
a strong shaft of sunlight, shining through from ear to ear,
illuminating the inside of my head, to very brightly hear,
an IQ with a minus sign right alongside it, on a good day,
a dizzy miss Lizzy/ an addled Harry, that's me in every way.

Christopher Higgins

THE 'OPTION' OF NO

Landmark familiar most welcome
When travelling home via the sea
Horizon white, the cliffs of Dover
Now fast becoming memory
Oblivion, modern day technology.

This island no longer protected
Seas whipping round coastline our shores
Channel Tunnel, popular opinion, invitation
Invasion pestilence disease, creeping
Through unseen loopholes unlocked doors.

We are British and proud of being so
Men women sons daughters, gave their lives
For this land, one time island sanctuary
Steeped in history, a jewel desired
By crowns, invading hordes
Ever watchful ever ambitious, the enemy.

Today without sense or reason
No battle campaign, course to win
Our future decided by *Word!* preposterously so
Public feeling excluded
No vote, no chance of saying no!

Our heritage you cannot wipe out
The British nature neither
Converted continentals with *Euro?*
Never! Sabotage, the inside ranks of glory
Elected egoists, refusing to listen
Duty forgotten, representation of the people
People, dismayed alarmed angry
Trust misplaced, missed chance
      'The option of *No*'

Mildred F Barney

LET LOOSE

The silence broke
though none had spoke
the atmosphere
had bled with fear
the whispers grew
that no one knew

how can this be
they asked of me
but I don't know
I told them so
then someone said
we'll all be dead

the radio
screamed time to go
prepare for Hell
someone yelled
the people cried
don't let us die

oh help us please
they begged of me
and I felt guilt
up to the hilt
why don't I know
I felt so low

I could not cope
and lost all hope
oh help me please
I'm on my knees
  ... the radio
  ... screamed time to go

James Reid

MATHEMATICS

For a while we made our equation new
We got the right solution
And all the routes led back to you
But given time formulas went astray
I needed a solution just to get from day to day

However, we found our love increased the population
This final output helped my reputation
The information of the equation being
I followed my heart, blindfold never seeing

The dangers I thought minute in proportion
Two new right-angled triangles couldn't be square
Thought if we added ourselves together
Then we might just get somewhere

Well my investigations are showing how
I was average in my needs and now
The tables have turned
My problems that you're not there at night
And the shape of things isn't looking bright

'Cos I love you, I find, now that we're divided
To the depth and breadth and height provided
We're at diagonals joined only by a thin line
In calculation, you're no longer mine.

Sharon Clarke

THE COMPUTER

It sits there this machine
The usurping power of the late 20th century
Man controls only by the on/off switch
Once on the global world is reduced
To a succession of coded statements
The terminology itself hints of another world, remoteness
Internet, log on, cyberspace web
So cold clinical and vapid
It lulls one into believing anything is available

The human hand unleashes the power
It lights up and all systems go
Log on into the World Wide Web www.
Correct page press icon
Like NASA preparing for lift-off
Enter name, password
Is there a communiqué
Yes
Receive - malfunction
Machine refuses to reveal

As time goes on
The human brain begins to understand
No longer fear
This non feeling cold machine
And takes control and solves the problems
Finally confirms
That as we into the 21st century go
The living are supreme

Moira H Thorburn

TIME OF CHANGE

Seen myself this thing called living seen myself
there's just no giving don't give up trying can't
you see we are just all dying.

Call it virtual reality it's complete insanity
trying to get out of this world we've messed up
taking drugs getting high lying around like
slugs waiting to die.

Too lazy to make the move knowing there's something
to prove worried about the way I look I know it's in the book
it's not no fairy tale, no way I'm getting out of this one on bail.

Forgetting about those who love me then
I've got to think of who's above me.
Following each other around like lost sheep not knowing
I am already in far too deep all this flirting all it's doing is hurting
everybody with their fingers in the pot.

Never thinking of the needy what have they got where will it
all end, one great day the angels he will send it won't be sad
for he will show us the difference between good and bad.

J P Smyth

BATTERED, SCATTERED - GOING THERE

There's a woman in a phone box,
She's crying out loud,
Tears slip off her face,
She thumps the glass, the pain.

People pass, people drive,
shifting their gears,
The noise all around her,
Silences the show.

Muffled communication,
Another language, alone,
And all the time in her panic,
The receiver dangles on the phone.

News connected by a wire,
But malfunction in her brain,
Means the translated messages,
Drive and drive insane.

Breaking down, folded up,
Wet from sweat and cries,
Emotional malfunction,
A victim, *'Abide'*.

```
        Without            conforming
                 To      a         role,
                             With     no
            need to          be
alone,
            a new,         a death,
                  a beginning,    an end,
                  The
                       long       last      means,
                                              To a
                  perfect
                                                friend.
```

Tom Scott

ULTIMATHE ULAE

He could hear the screaming on the wind,
The anguish of a million voices,
Some angry, some pleading
But all in vain,
They are not ghosts
They are spirits of the earth
Defenders of Mother Nature

And he? What is he?
A scientist, who devotes his life
To the betterment of mankind,
So why do the voices torment him so?
He has the backing of
many learned men of science,
And the government itself

Everybody knows that GMO is safe,
Everyone, that is, who matters,
Pesticides have been in use for years,
The corncrake was a small price to pay,
- for cheaper food,
And as for BSE,
Well that wasn't his fault, was it?

Still the voices come to him,
And always on the wind
He puts his torment down
to overwork and fatigue,
As he takes yet more steps
Down the dark dusty road,
And ignores the screaming on the wind

__Mandy Holten__

NATIVES

Shepherded into corners;
lands and lives stolen
futures killed off
homes taken;
making room for machines
ancestors turning in graves not knowing
where to visit those left behind

Beauty desecrated
children torn from parents
Desolate villages the lost signs of the life
of people once so strong; so proud
They cared for the land; respected each other
Now they're betrayed by false words
from men who don't care

Scotland; America; Australia as well
stripped bare of land; homes; pride
Bowed under the foot of the strong men from hell
Greedy hands striking children down
raping the women; defiling the land

Natives forever banned from their lands
Never to be allowed pride in their cultures
No more building homes for the children
No farming to feed their wives
Ruled for all time by tyrants and braggarts

Who gave them the right to lay claim to the land
What edict allows them to throw others out
Where came the ideas of owning the land
which was given in trust for men to respect
presented as a blessed gift to us all
to be shared by all those who live
all those who toil
to the natives who cared

Fiona Higgins

I Give You Science

Scientifically serious, all reasoning, all searching.
Scientifically senseless, lifting and lurching
Trying to touch the bowels of the earth,
Trying to reach the limits of the sky.
Building, encasing, cocooning and lacing,
Concocting machinery out of future dreams
For rushing here or transporting there.
A life of perfection in one direction.
Encasing the wind, redirecting the moon,
Obliterating the sun, forgetting the world.
Destroying for greed the things we need.
A plastic, manic, insensitive army
Of mass media, surging with the tide,
Emblazoned with logos and burned with back-packs,
Conditioned by computers, with freedom limited.
A push button world with minds infiltrated.
Awareness a myth, arrogance a gift.
Let's continue to alter, never mind the risk
And change this world to a cold, hard disc,
Not soft and round, but flattened and bound.
Smashed by the force of man's forward course
Into a future of plastic containers,
Of machine mania and soulless bodies,
No reaping, no sowing, no planting, no mowing,
A clinical world of locks and clocks,
A future where you'll have the choice
To drift in space or watch the box.
I give you science . . . it's yours!

Joan E Blissett

SPECKS OF DUST

Why in the world
Do we think ourselves important?
In the vastness of the universe
We are minute specks,
Inconsequential as the dust
That wafts across the arching sky.
Even a hover-fly,
Busy in its little life,
Has more purpose to it
Than all of humankind.
We are inflated in our pride,
Yet transient as pollen on the breeze.

Jean Oxley

Millennium Vacancy

There's a vacancy as the century ends.

An ache in the soul, not dissimilar to a boil
without pus, an empty dome, a carbuncle,
that casts a shadow of oppression on the spirit.
There's nothing to fill the shallowness only,
gaudy goods, the apotheosis, of an economic miracle.

The decline of a civilisation.

It's easy to drown in the shallowness
because there is no breath in a spirit
that no longer seeks, only an ache in the soul
without an anodyne for an anorexic age.

It's not even easy to overdose.

Standing on the apex of the end.
Peering with eyes squinted towards the future,
there's nothing to prophosize, nothing to see.
It's enough to shout out Jeezus.
There's not even an echo.

Roman Suchyj

MY HOPE

If this life is the only time
we live, and when we die
there's nothing more, let's wine and dine
and never question *why!*

Some spend their years acquiring wealth,
or idly waste their time;
Whilst others concentrate on health,
or seeking power through crime.

No thought of what may be in store
when life's brief journey ends.
Just live for gain - ignore the poor,
too late to make amends.

This life is just a vapour
when placed within God's plan.
It's vital that you ponder
before you reach your span.

Now I believe our life goes on
where here we breathe no more.
And I thank God He sent His son
to open Heaven's door.

I know not why He made the way
for sinners to be saved.
I only know I could not pay
for my sins to be waived.

You smile and think I am insane
to believe God sent the Light.
You may believe my hope is vain,
but just suppose I'm right.

Joan Picton

CARELESS!

How often has it been said, certainly not rare
that each life should be filled with loving care.
One then can only guess as we survey the mess,
accompanied by distress
As we cover and recover the ground,
but it still cannot be found.

Does it leave you in despair? Was it on the piano?
The table or a chair?
You thought you left it there!
No! Then you left it where?
I may not even guess
Good job we have an extra pair,
did you make the usual mistake?
Would it be just and fair you failed to live your life with care,
unless you became confused by the care you used.
Need I further stress?
The care you used became confused, by sheer carelessness!

Benny Howell

As To Smiling At Work...

With a determined smile you face the day
Only to have it eroded away
At nine it's fine
At ten it's a grin
At eleven it's thin
At twelve, like this poem it's going
At one the cracks are showing
At two the strain is growing
At three after tea a small sign of recovery
At four you can't smile much more
At five it's barely alive
At six as you walk out the door, it falls to the floor.

Robert Denis Spencer

FREEDOM OF CHOICE

Will only death bring peace to we
condemned to pay for BBC.
We, who must survive on lowly pay
live to dread each new-born day.

Our dwindling funds extorted by the law
that feeds the rich and keeps us poor.
While, those who shelter in this mammoth club
beyond the streets where shoulders rub.
Do criticise and give offence
with half-brained wits who make no sense.

They cater us with filth and porn
treat us like the devil's spawn;
No comedy without more smut
as if all life did ought but rut.
No play without the bedroom sight
of sex, without the dark of night.

Have pity on the mass in need
who now so low on blood to bleed.
To bolster puppets, dull to eyes, so tired
of trash, repeats the uninspired.
Enough to make the public offer prayer
for swift release from wear and tear;
inflicted by a feudal law.
Pay up, or face the reaching claw
of those who have for those without
a way to cast protesters out.

Commercialise this giant drain
make it work to keep it's gain.
Not coddle those of little worth;
make them earn their place on earth.
As we, without the helping hand
to give us lifestyles over grand.

'Tis we, the public pay the keep
whose purse-string wide by reaching deep;
And we, the ones to have the right
to pull the purse-strings close and tight.

Henry J Green

WORKHORSE

Body jerks
  Alarm blasting
    Eyes blink Once Twice
      Dumb blind foot finds stirrup
        Hoisting into saddle Stomach not up yet
          Whistle blowing Steelhorse kicking
            Speeding up now
              Perniciously consuming life

                    Perhaps we should
                      Work less Play more
                      Barter Community-serve
                      Create Think
                      Rest more Love more
                      Fulfil oneself

              Office stuffy
            Open window
        Noise pollution Thick gut fumes
      Boss right You wrong Do as you're told
    Tiring not being yourself Drag-day over
Growing dimpse home again sleep
D
 I
  S
   M
    O
     U
      N
       T

Barbara Dudley

POETS OF TODAY

Poets of today are figments of the modern theme
Full of millennium ideas to make the world sit up
No more bungling of this and that
Fishing around like an old rheumatic prat
Wondering whether the poet world will agree
With what one has written to the right degree
Thank goodness the ancient poetry way has been shelved
We modern poets are now free to be ourselves.

Alma Montgomery Frank

Hmmm... Well!

Heaven to Eternity
Space to infinity.

> Life after death
> Life before
>
> A source of being that precipitates back and forth

Which will it be?
Could it be both!

Mike Bradley

THE UNFORTUNATE

For all it's worth there's still a smile
from the day of love of a laughing child.
But when she opens her eyes, with inevitable cries
for the chaos she sees comes of no surprise.
It knows no better and has seen no worse,
our cruel world is now her Earth.
Senseless as it seems, she begins to talk,
then learns and thinks and ventures to walk.

For you can't stop the process, you can't even warn,
even though you know that she will come to harm.
If only her education would come a little soon,
and then maybe she'd never wish to leave her room.

Steven Jenkins (19)

STREET CODE

I follow the code
The code of the street.
The slang
The dress sense
The hard-core beat.
I'm not an American
I don't own a gat
But I know where it's at
I play football
To my heart's content
Go to night clubs
To get some love
But sometimes when push comes to shove
All life seems pointless
I never lay back
I stand upright
And follow the *streetcode!*

Trevor Hussey

You?

They are conjuring up an image of the way that life should be.
The only problem being that it isn't right for me.
I see the bigger picture, not the trademark or the price.
We should not be identical like tiny grains of rice.
Not white, nor bland. Not uniform, nor clones of an idolised few.
Look inside your heart and find the strength to let out You.
For buried beneath the commercialism where your identity used to be
is a tiny trembling shadow that really must be freed.
Freed to see the sun rise, and to dream beneath stars.
Freed to be beautiful despite, height or weight or scars.
Freed to dance without a tune, to love without its fears,
to sing, to live without the guilt, and with only laughter's tears.
So close your eyes and open your mind remembering your
shadow's still weak, but listen very carefully and allow
your soul to speak.

Angel Blue

SENSITIVE SIREN

Inside, tight, breathe
Thin, want to
emerge.
        Cannot well
          then experience
             nothing.
Enjoy, emptiness,
        This, sensitive siren
        just goes off!
        Loud and alarming
             in depths of
             some body
             is it
             mine!

Lesley Lewis

STANDING ON THE EDGE OF THE WORLD

Far southwards in Antarctica a polar gulf is forming,
A deeper chill is permeating known as global warming.
The tolling bell of progress peels out its sombre chime
Above the frozen wilderness of glaciated time.

The result of modern living doesn't need too much researching,
Our environment is under siege, its very soul is hurting.
Man's hectic quest for power over Nature's slower ways
Grows ever more frenetic and is this the price he pays?

The blame lies with each one of us as on the fence we're sitting,
Our guiltiness is by default, our greed we're not admitting.
We won't go without our motor cars, give up our flights abroad,
We'll *pay* to save the world of course, our time we *can't* afford.

We know that in the scheme of things someone must do some thinking,
It can't be me, it must be you whose fault it is we're sinking.
The sun descends, the oceans ebb, but will they flow again;
The moon and stars are beckoning - tomorrow's world for men?

Our future's here beneath our feet, we won't concede it's dying,
Mankind's inventions *can* recoup if only we keep trying.
We've raced along the lemming path and now we're on a ledge -
We need a hand to save our world from falling off the edge.

Coral Spark

THERE'S NO JOY ON THOSE STREETS!

All is black, grey or white
where once the sky was blue.
Where colours once abounded.

Hope is mustered in that constant line
just one day's work for mere survival.
No work! Becomes the sound's addiction.

I beg the power for drink's sweet escape
shared with other souls fallen from grace.
Swigged bottled fire, an exit from this
skidded row, till colour is reborn.

Cars reduce their speed for eyes to gaze
disgust at my degradation.
Pathetic circus that life churns up.
Could it be that I was once like you?

They carry bags back home. Bags with food.
Back to home. Gone. Destroyed my Temple.
No strength to cope life's complexities.

I stand in file for Mission Food
Pay price with mandatory prayer.
On street once more to *walk, walk and walk*
No shelter from rain's sky.

Inescapable void where life has deposited me.

A bench becomes a haven. Respite
for wearied bones to doze into oblivion.

I find a shelter. Protection from night
Pungent with disinfectant, to disguise
the smell of vomit. Uncontrolled urine.

Grey rules posted upon grey walls.
Hushed ravings from strange bedfellows.

Is there no release from these streets?

Leslie Fine

THE ENEMY WITHIN

Your fear entwines, like the pattern on the wall.
Standing as one, yet so isolated.
It peers at you
Studying you through the barred
Cage of your desire.

Remember trying to enter, trying to face the beast inside.
The eyes of experience thrashing your courage.
Defeating your strength
And burning up the last hope of
Standing your enemy.

We avoid the Almighty, the hidden horror behind the facade.
It hides now and settles in.
No longer abusing you.
But it always will entwine you and
Hold you as prisoner.

Alexis Stearns

FACADE

Where have all the good ones gone?
Have they sold out to something, I could never belong.
Where have all my good friends gone?
Well, they said it for something and that something was wrong
But I need to stop this thinking
In this solitary state of mind
Where does all the truth belong?
Well, I thought that pure honesty could never be wrong.
Where have all the wise men gone?
Well, they're talking for nothing and they're not even strong.
And they need to stop their preaching
When their people are walking blind
And there's no room left for feeling
When their thoughts are just left to die.
Where has all the goodness gone?
If we show some emotion, they forget who we are.
Where have all the righteous gone?
If they show any virtue it's been taken too far.
But they need to stop pretending
'Cos the life we all see is lies
And there's always time for making
Any changes before we die.
Where did your life seem to go?
After all you had created just became a *one man show*.
Thought that you could never lose
'Til your day of judgement surfaced and your time arrived to choose.
So you need to stop denying
'Cos reality finds it's way
And you may as well stop trying
To be more than the role you play.

Caroline J Sammout

NIGHT THOUGHTS

It's quiet and still I can feel the chill.
The tunnel is dark not even a spark.
They say there's a light it's nowhere in sight.
Many books I have read lying sleepless in bed.
That's not strictly true I just skim them through.
Thoughts on other things
Wondering what morning brings.
Dawn will finally break and I'm still awake.
I get up and dress don't I look a mess.
God! Look at my hair do I really care?
No need for show I've nowhere to go.
No work anymore they've shown me the door.
I thought I'd be glad
- but -
Retirement is sad!

Betty Harness

THE BEST OF BRITISH

Oh! for the British banger
Roast beef and Yorkshire pud.
Devonshire scones complete cream teas
In Scotland it's shortbread.

The joy of each new season
God given for us to enjoy.
The joy of new-born lambs - the golden daffodils.
That purple-headed mountain covered
With heather and bracken
Wearing at times a shroud of cloud
In winter it's white snow.

The singing and bringing into our gardens
of the youngest of the birds.
The robin, wren, tits and blackbird
The sparrows always there.

Sweet scent of English roses
Honey suckle mingling in the hedgerows.
In the Autumn cobwebs will follow
Sparkling with frost till it disappears.

Gone are the days, when we used to ride by tram.
Iron with old flat irons, heated by what means we could.
Maypole dancers - Morris men still they come and go.
Remembered with affection, in British spring and summer days.

But, God's work in all its glory, is here to stay for us.
The babbling brook, changing shadows on the mountain top.
Bright sunshine in a little bit of Heaven
They were all given by him above, for us.

Heather D Hill

The Best Of British

Forget about the ban on beef
forget about the Euro.
Just remember, patriotism, traditions,
Land of Hope and Glory, that tiny island,
set in a silver sea.
The beating heart of London.
The flowing River Thames.
Red double-decker buses, running
up and down, passing ancient land-marks
of history, old and new.
Wren's wedding cake steeple of St Bride,
in it's crypt, an old Roman wall.
Westminster, touched by many Kings.
Marking the Great Fire of 1666,
the monument on Pudding Lane.
Nash laid out Trafalgar Square,
where Nelson stands on high.
Then take a taxi, up the Mall
passing under Marble Arch, to see the Queen,
passing Queen Victoria, sixty years she reigned.
Back to the west end, theatres by the score.
Along the river bank, Festival Hall.
Shakespeare's Globe, history indeed.
Cross the river to the Tower,
where many a head did roll, the list goes on and on . . .
But let us stop, and remember history new,
the bombs that showered down on you.
Your spirit they could not kill.
Never surrender, always be,
the Best of British, we can be.

Audrey Allen

THE NIGHT RAID

They came again in the night
In the darkness lit by fire
And shattered our day-long peace.
The hoard of casual killers
Come nightly to destroy us all
And beat us to surrender.
They thunder 'cross the busy sky
Seeking targets innocent.
Of harming them as they fly
Until the fighters fall on them
And nipping, biting, tearing them
As they fight back with all they have
By the night sky terriers,
Though few, they kill and kill
As the clumsy bombers try
To turn for home and safety
Leaving destruction and the dead
In cities still defiant.

Richard Reeve

THE BEST OF BRITISH

A family like ours would cease to be
But for the benefit of a transplant and a craniotomy.
A triple by-pass and a laparotomy
Three cheers for the National Health.

Much maligned and criticised
Under-staffed and under subscribed.
Nye Bevan's vision realised
Three cheers for the National Health.

Our unborn babies monitored
With latest high technology.
Looked after from cradle to the grave,
Three cheers for the National Health.

And we in turn salute it
Throughout its great complexity,
And changing market strategy,
Three cheers for the National Health.

Beryl Moorehead

BEST OF BRITISH

Land of hope, land of mystery,
Steeped in legend, soaked in history.
Arthurian legend in search of the Grail
Romance versus gallantry - a worthy tale.
Stonehenge - misty mystery,
Burial mounds - archaeology of our history.
Romans and Vikings charged our coastal sand,
Brave warriors in battle defend the land.
Pomp and ceremony, hard to beat
A royal wedding, a special treat.

Learned men of yesteryear
Inventors, builders, skilled in career.
Code-breakers, Spitfire makers
For them all we do cheer.
Oxford and Cambridge battle on
Eton and Sandhurst sing victory song.
The Morris dancers with their bells and bows
Slap thighs whilst dancing on their toes.
Trumpets, bugles of the brass band,
Tradition, culture, steeped in this land.

Ruth Wright

BEST OF BRITISH

What is it that makes Britain great?
Our country, now a member state.

Here, railways now worldwide began
Invented by a British man.

Britain found her own solution
With the industrial revolution.

Our NHS we all applaud,
There's nothing like it yet, abroad.

Royal pageants, dated they may be,
But many tourists come to see.

Then what makes Britain beautiful?
Our artists may be dutiful.

Yorkshire Dales, a leafy lane,
Wooded vales, soft summer rain.

The wide, green downs, undulating
And blossom trees where wild birds sing.

Scottish mountains towering high,
Raising peaks up to the sky.

Country village with rippling stream
Where one can sit and laze and dream.

What makes Britain interesting,
That tourists come, winter and spring?

Her towns and cities full of life,
Where people dwell through joy and strife.

Historic castles, firm and strong,
Standing through the years so long.

The London theatres, famous stars
And social groups in clubs and bars.

Winters may bring rain, hail or snow
But there is nowhere else I'd go.

Jeanne Ison

MADE IN BRITAIN

Land of culture, land of grace.
This regal isle, this special place.
How can I encapsulate
All that has made Britain great?

William Shakespeare, Nelson's fleet
221b Baker Street.
The Tower of London and Big Ben,
Henry the Eighth and Sir Christopher Wren.

Byron, Dickens, Browning, Scott,
The Battle of Hastings, the Gunpowder Plot,
Gainsborough, Constable, Shelley and Clare,
'The Thirty Nine Steps' and 'Vanity Fair.'

Oscar Wilde and Rupert Brooke
Sir Francis Drake and Captain Cook,
Filtered sunshine through the trees
And haunting Elgar melodies.

'Brief Encounter' - 'The Cruel Sea'
Peter Cushing and Christopher Lee.
Rolling hills, a shower of rain,
The Beatles, Bond and Michael Caine.

'Genevieve' - 'Hancock's Half Hours'
Ealing films and Fawlty Towers,
Henry Cooper, Stirling Moss,
The British Legion, The Victoria Cross.

Echoes of a glorious past
Serve only to inspire and cast
The shadow of their aspirations
Across the future generations.

P R Canham

MADE IN ENGLAND

When spanners were spanners and never wrenches,
When manuals spoke of mudguards, not of fenders,
Oiled mechanics toiled on sturdy, Sheffield benches.

Under an empire sky, Lucas lit the wet leafy lanes,
Albion cogs coupled compression, clocking up the miles,
An industrial hey-day past but still the glory remains.

Carborundum ground valves, huff and puff vaporised powers,
Co-ordinated con rods rise and fall with mechanical precision,
Cotter pins, smoothly coerced into scorching tubular towers.

When midland forges raged and roared with pride,
When chrome was plated in a thickness to endure,
An expanding two wheel industry began to thrive.

Birmingham turned from small arms to make its marque,
Nottingham delivered the humble Raleigh,
Then Turner's Coventry twins were up and sung with the lark.

Braised, bolted and bent, drilled, tapped, turned and milled,
The British motor cycle engineers created their legend,
A machine from a great nation, made by a people highly skilled.

The often eccentric few, kept the breed of iron running,
Till at last in Triumph, a new-fashioned era is coming,
T prefixed triples on the Queen's highway, engines humming.

Charles Green

IN MY DAY

What was it like to live in my day
to me it was perfect in every way.
Candlelight burning not very bright
but no electric to give us more light.

No television to take up our time
conversation we had at your place and mine.
Boredom was something we never knew
or standing for hours in a queue.

Walking through fields with flowers so bright
watching them close their eyes for the night.
So quiet and peaceful long ago
those were the days I remember so.

Life today is much too fast
sitting in cars just driving past.
No time to stop and say hello
the more they learn the less they know.

Respect was something we were taught
to care for others when help is sought.
Today I see them turn away
life is sad since my young day.

Sometimes I think of long ago
when times were hard and life was slow.
But love and care I have to say
that's what I learned back in my day.

Florence Davies

Victim TV

Bring your dirty linen to me
and I'll make you a star.
As long as you dredge up all your secrets
and rip open your scars.

It doesn't matter who you hurt
the public have a right to know.
Adultery, love triangles and sham marriages
we'll put you straight on our show.

Just cry for the camera
and we'll do the rest.
'You're a natural honey.
You won't need make-up
to look a mess.'

We'll arrange a surprise visit
from a relative you never knew you had.
For extra publicity and viewers
how about a seance with your dad?

Whether the guests are fake or real
who the hell cares.
It's a done deal
a bit of drama for your dull day.
Just don't believe
anything you hear or see.
Smile, this isn't Candid Camera
you're on *Victim TV!*

Sean Brown

TODAY'S WORLD

Rush and noise, horns that blare,
flashing lights with brilliant glare.
No-one stays still for a minute
but tries to cram so many things in it.
Disco dancing and the gym,
working, shopping and any passing whim.
Can't stop to chat - haven't the time,
run down the street, wave and mime
To friends that I used to know and love,
when did I last visit - heavens above
It must have been two years ago,
Their father died and they were feeling low,
have I really reached a stage when I don't care,
No time to see what's really there.
Where have I gone, is this really me,
rushing from place to place that I never see,
The things and people once I treasured,
their value to me could never be measured.
Please forgive me for all the awful neglect,
I really had no intention those I valued to reject,
I just felt so pressured by the world around,
but now on reflection I have found
that fads and whims don't mean a lot
and I find I'm so grateful for what I've got.
I now have contentment and peace of mind
and friends mean so much more to me I find.
Oh that others might realise and see
for all that activity, their lives are so empty.

Doris I Livesey

JUSTICE FOR STEPHEN LAWRENCE

I ask
What is justice for blacks if like Stephen Lawrence you're a
victim of a brutal and fatal crime in this country.
Does the police force bluntly turn the tables in confrontation.
Fail in acting upon vital clues and critical information.
Wait idly around for weeks before investigating and taking
any lines of action.
Giving the perpetrators enough time to destroy at their own
leisure, the incriminating evidence and to create and mould the
perfect alibi's in concrete.
Frighten and intimidate the witnesses so they are no longer
prepared, out of fear, to give statements.
By which time the entire case comes collapsing down to its
ashamed knees.

Meanwhile someplace else, five smug racist thugs with no
hint of guilt or remorse - walk free, having made a mockery
of what is known as the British justice system.
Clear in the arrogant knowledge that they've escaped justice
at the hands of police corruption.
Then the same hypercritical system slams repeatedly every avenue
and option that was once open and available for the Lawrence family
to pursue.

Maybe it was the intense media circus and public outcry that resulted
in the wake of some kind of blame amongst all its denials being
shouldered in this case, whilst many others before had been ignored.
But even with all this public interest and support all of Stephen's
murderers cannot be convicted in the court of law.

Is this what they call justice I ask, if you're black and a victim
of crime in this country?

Saheeda Khan

Mask

Nails are breaking off;
the face will be next.
I can see it now:
it hits the floor,
cracks and wrecks;
the perfect paintwork
that's been practised for hours.

Peeling and flaking
slowly revealing
a pair of eyes
hiding from the world.
The secret's out,
what they wanted to know:
The hidden agenda of a patchwork girl.

Liana Cougar

APOCALYPSE

My world being destroyed above and below
how far are they prepared to go?
Destroying my world surrounded with wonder.
Pollutants bring violent storms tremendous thunder.
Seasons mixed up, mother nature forgets
when it should be dry, when it should be wet.
Cars - bumper to bumper, pollute my fresh air
Breath in and out as car fumes you share.
Rainforest you savagely plunder,
relentless scramble to obtain more lumber.
My leafy lane I once walked with pride,
strewn with rubbish from either side.
Russian children disfigured from radiation,
yet we still prepare for millennium celebration.
Whole countries destroyed by overwhelming tides.
Earthquake victims, homeless - their loved ones died.
Mountains of rubbish voil blot on the land.
Ocean's filthy sewage lies on freshly washed sand.
Politicians lost their way through corruption and greed.
Yet thousands on Mother Earth we need to feed.
God created a world so full of wonder
in return we mistreat, pillage we plunder.
The millennium draws ever near
should we rejoice or should we fear.
Mankind's gone too far of this I am certain
Mankind reflect - could this be our final curtain?

Ann Hathaway

VICTORIA FALLS

On the Zambezi River
Victoria Falls.

Deep into Africa
the magic roars.

Powerful and strong
yet elegant and graceful.

Falling to the river
from which it came.

Like its country
flowing freely in harmony.

The people of Africa
best they forget.
The hatred and racism.

Victoriously destroyed
by the true beauty
of Africa.

The People . . .

Lee Round

HOPES AND DREAMS
(Inspired by Rob Frost's Hopes & Dreams Millennium Concert)

Young men seeing visions
The old dreaming dreams.
Our prayers for the future
Now the theme of all schemes.

A yearning for world peace
A land free from strife
Each man happy to live
With one partner, his wife.

Where children are blessings
Loved, taught and well-fed.
Nurtured, tended, sheltered
With a home and a bed.

All sick folk looked after
Their pain eased by prayer
The welfare of others
Being first point of care.

The trees, meadows, flowers
Lakes, rivers, streams.
Flourishing, replenished
By God's Grace in these dreams.

A millennium thought -
that all lands review.
A new walk with Jesus -
Hopes and dreams can come true!

Joan Heybourn

A Single Mother's Dream

Once the morning sun had rose in the sky,
Like a zombi she opened her eyes.
After stretching her arms and legs,
her necessity to work, she vacated her bed.
While the wind on her window, played Jacob's tune
another strenuous day, had come too soon.
She washed and fed her children
to school, they would go.
Her housework completed, a part-time job she too must go.
Working, family feeding many debts to pay
her leisure-time, soon passes away.
If she was a millionaire, in the sun, she could lie,
dark glasses, would keep the sun from her eyes.
A housemaid, and nannie, she could hire
from this human rat race, she would retire . . .

B Marshall

Moving

The frightened child
forlorn and angry
standing behind me
rummaging inside me.

Away, away,
yet how to free myself
I do not know;
maybe time is unredeemable indeed;
you and me welded together
inseparable in our fear.

But I am. Now.

Andrea Kenkmann

COME WITH ME, LOVE

Come with me, love, so gently thru the mist
      — Our faithful ally, blacking out the light
From stars above — to where we two once kissed
      In secret on a kindred starless night
And there, beneath the branches of the willow
      Keeping us lost to all the world we'll lie
In ecstasy — a bed of moss our pillow!
      A hidden chamber safe from ev'ry eye
Save of the night-bird; of the cricket-choir
      The silent, sightless bat; the firefly
Whose pulsing lamp speaks of a like desire
      All but a portion of Night's tender charms
Yet I'll be conscious only of your arms
      Drawing my naked body towards your own
Enfolding me completely in such bliss
      The like of which my heart has never known
But dreamt of daily since that one, sweet kiss
      Beneath the willow tree so long ago
So soft my darling, come away with me
      To lie in love until the first cock's crow
— To where our pining spirits will be free
      To roam, enrapt'd, the realms of reverie.

Michael Pendragon

RESURRECTION

She lies there!
In Sleepy Hillock Cemetery;
Her grave unkempt and bare . . .
Damn the poverty!
No mark . . .
Just grooves!
The grief -
The memory -
The defeat -
The despair!
The utter disbelief!
All alone . . .
Until the rain dries;
And the snow melts;
And the frost is gone;
And the shadow moves,
And a lark begins to rise
So sweet against the air!

Tom Ritchie

An Age-Old Abortion

Blood stringy and a brightening red.
Warm, too warm
Scolding, bubbling
As my womb pulses it out
I'm crying to the animals
Hiding in far away
Here to be alone, to bury it
And decay away in that hole.
I think I dreamt him
Cold and hard through the
Billowing curtains
Always gone when the heat crawls in
The air dies down,
I'm left sweating to sheets
Damp everywhere, leaking him
Onto my sheets
His lips, his touch
Stay all day, highlighting the world
Smiling,
Laughter
All my own contagious
I wonder where he is now
Leaving me alone
The grass itching my red flesh
Sun drains my energy
I'm limp
Exhausted
Strained out
It all comes
Glistening and mucky
Blood-streaked
We cried together
Laying
Waited
I drag myself up
My body just sweat

I wash
Listening to the baby cry
In a pool of muddy water
I dig a hole
My hands are red and blistered
Nails full and raised
With dirt
There's water down there
Sticking mud to me
I killed my baby
With a rock
Sharp, jutted
With tinier stones inside
I buried that too
Nothing remained
Once I ripped up the grass
A reef for my baby
Covering his pink face
Sliding off his bloated belly
I shoved the earth
Onto him
Packed tight
So no one would think to look
I dressed and went back home.

August Head

DYSFUNCTION JUNCTION

Joyboy's in the lounge, resting 'tween parties,
poppin' pills he keeps in a packet of Smarties.
Work gets in the way so he's on the dole,
a Party Professional Life and Soul.
Drinks till he's sick, thinks with his dick,
acts as if he's as thick as a brick.
Along the line, he's lost his personality,
in a fight to fit in it's another fatality.
He'll only say I love you when completely fried,
and never let you know of all the tears he's cried.

It's just another night at Dysfunction Junction.

Up in her room is Lady Scream-Queen,
Stands before her mirror practising looking obscene.
Dressed in black with a face like an albino,
drinking cheap booze that's unfit for a wino.
Mood swings from psychotic to morose,
trying to stop anyone getting too close.
How could she stand another's affection,
when she revolts at the sight of her own reflection?
So she screams and shouts, bathes in self-doubts,
and covers it up with her lipstick pouts.

It's just another night at Dysfunction Junction.

Geekfreak's playing truth or dare with his demons,
ignoring the stench of his blood and semen.
Enough smack in his arm to launch him to the moon,
he sits and spins a bottle in the night-time gloom.
His devils tell him truths he doesn't want to hear,
while he shivers in the clutches of a drug-felled fear.
The line between truth and lie becomes blurred,
and he starts to distrust each and every word.
His eyes open wider than ever before,
knife enters his chest and he breathes no more.

Could you see the morning at Dysfunction Junction?

Aron M Smith

TIME BEING

Waken me, dear child,
Ere chance should wash my soul
In final memories,
And this poor state would leave me
Only painful recollections
Of past joys and sins.

Transcend regrets;
Mistaken harbour for this aching heart,
And let me see
Each instant of sad memory extolled;
Compressed in scenes as real
As liquid dreamscapes
Truth revealed.

For dreams are all
This dear existence, omnipresent
Ever meant to be;
And timeless effort, seemingly eternal,
Blends its history
Into the substance of my total being,
And fades from me.

D A Warren

MY LOVER AND ME

The moist sea air I feel on my face
As my lover takes me to our special place
His eyes do shine like stars in space
Such beauty I have never seen in any
                             other face . . .

The warmth of his tender embrace
My heart starts to beat at a rapid pace
His love for me and passionate desire
Overwhelms me like a heavenly choir
For this is the man that God ordained
To look on me as his best friend.

Who would have known that it was the plan
That God created woman for man
And such a delight she would be
He'd be singing God's praises eternally.

Helen Jane Bailey

FALLING APART

The spring turns into winter so onwards we merrily go.
Summer flowers lose their glaze, under a pile of snow.
The fleecy lambs grow and mature, cutlets upon a plate.
Such is the rolling canopy of clouds overseeing our fate.

We try to ignore failing signs as horrid wrinkles appear.
The shrinking hair shades to grey while teeth disappear.
The chassis that we once cherished shows signs of rust.
God help us, but visible to perceive, is the sagging bust!

Jumping out of bed early mornings is a hit upon the floor.
Failing hamstring muscles signal, we'll crawl to the door.
Lacing up shoes requires a stoop, rightly a mammoth task.
Straightening up a mirror winks, sadly in need of a mask!

Our skin is taut. Weakening eyes shun the sparkle of life.
Years of neglect twisted us into a real contortion of strife.
Instead of being proactive, we're reactive to sad extreme.
Tiring minds ignore this dichotomy, so difficult to gleam!

T Burke

THE LAWYER - MRS ROSEMARY NELSON

Black flags on the lamp posts
Death has left his grizzly mark
More blood spilled in the road
That leaves the future looking dark

Red hands with the devil's work
A bomb beneath a car
And peace is something still to reach
That lies somewhere afar

Threats, then Justice murdered
And an ill wind's anger blows
Sends rioters upon the streets
Frustration overflows

A woman feared by loyalists
And strong arms of the law,
For defending human rights,
Abuse of which she did abhor.

Kim Montia

CONFIDENCE

Gosh, where do you buy this stuff?
Does it come in a packet or a tin?
I've asked everyone where to get it
They don't understand and grin!

Does it make you look better,
Or does it make you fat?
But it brings a sparkle to life,
I've heard about it, that's a fact!

Perhaps that's why they've sold out,
When will they have more in store?
Can't keep up with production,
Must be a headache for sure!

Ann Beard

CONFUSION

It is hard to describe the way I feel,
In a way for you to know it is for real,
My head it is spinning, round and around,
Making me lose my spiritual ground,
I need support, I feel so lost,
Which way to turn, whatever the cost,
I know life is precious, family and friends are too,
I have lost a link, one that holds it all together,
Is it a vision, a dream, or surreal?
I think it is time to open my heart,
The pain and the fear is tearing me apart,
I have cried so many tears, I do not know which door,
Which one is the right one, there are so many more,
If evil is a factor, from things in the past.
Then the fault is mine, but it cannot last,
Ouija, or magic, tarot, occult, let the way into my heart,
Turning, distorting, the truth and which path,
The spiritual battle goes on and on,
Mixed with life, battles feel like a bomb,
About to go off - and then be gone!
That is how I feel, is it so wrong?
I have lost the truth from fiction and fact,
Someone come and help me to stay here intact.

Gillian Weaving

HANDS OFF OUR POUND!

They can keep their beastly Euro, and leave us with our Pound,
There's too much interference, our heads are going round.
The French say 'Vive la difference', and we should say it too
And be happy to remember who won at Waterloo!
It isn't far from Brussels, which is where they hold the power
To tell us what we ought to do, the taste is rather sour.
A United States of Europe- is that right for you and me?
Of course not, what we need today, is a land that's really free.
Away with these restrictions, we've enough here of our own
So they can keep their Euro, and leave our Pound alone!

Rosa Riley

A Friend Concerned

Confide in me
When you've been driven too far down the colliding crossroad
of no return
And the shattering way ahead only leaves you feeling trapped inside
a bottle with nothing to learn
And all your whirlwind avenues you feel are expelled and burnt
So when your winding days and drifting nights are dark and lonely
And the fiery sun and moon continue to enslave your heart so it cannot
chime its song
Take me in your intensity of search as a friend concerned
Take my hand and together we'll dare to fly high on the open wings of a
weaving bird
We'll travel far and wide
Until all those trailing thoughts surrender to infinity
And your dust-filtered eyes can once again witness the victorious sunset
at each twisting turn
So rest assured
That in the ruffling wind I shall not pass disjointed judgement upon you
For it is no whispered or forsaken crime
For the sweet waters of your life to be blighted with pain and doubt
For every life has an unlucky night somewhere along the line
So when twilight flames circle to expose a scenery of smoke leaving
your vision blurred
Reach out to take me in the morning stead as a friend concerned.

Saheeda Khan

SHE

She walks the streets alone.
She does it every night,
she has no friends, no life.
She stands on her own two feet,
supporting herself.
She is always busy sitting down
writing poems and letters to
the people whom she walked out on.

But she will never send them
She says she will, but never
gets round to it.

She has all the time in the world,
she sits there watching all the
people walk past her.
She just looks at them and laughs,
and gets on with her own life
doing her own thing.

Chantelle Patterson

THE YUPPY

He really makes us moan
When he's on his fancy phone
The Yuppy.
And we love to send him far
In his big flash car
The Yuppy.
And I don't give a hoot
For his fancy suit
The Yuppy.
You're just a naughty puppy
You're a loud-mouthed Yuppy.

Colin Allsop

THE TWENTY-FIRST CENTURY

England, they say you are dying,
The long men from across the waters,
The small men behind the mountains,
The fearful, the proud, the scornful.
Do you hear them?
They say you are dying.
Your treasure slipping with scarcely a sigh
Out of your weary fingers.
And long built-up hopes,
Empiric glory,
The jewels of generations,
Sliding and slipping,
Crumbling down to nothing;
Grown old, feeble and useless.
Do you hear them?
They say you are dying.

Oh passionate flame
Flaring up in the darkness,
Driving the crawling shadows
Headlong out of the sky.
Driving the creeping mists
From the long-forgotten valleys,
Warming the cold grey earth
Into ecstasy.
Burn deeper into my heart like fires of old
Lit on windy hills to give the alarm,
Till all England awakened watchful,
Ready and strong to fight.
This is the twenty-first Century.
This is our age.

D S M

LAST RING CALL FOR SLAPSTICK CLOWNS

Since the middle of the fifties,
Slapstick clowning's largely faded.
Laugher response to spilt gunge, and
Custard pies is, really, jaded.

German ex-patriot Carl
Brenner recalls early contacts
With Coco, while he was learning.
Both favoured the *messy* acts.

I don't care how long his shirt took
To put on; but that clown's brother
Pulled it out - while walking from
One ring-wall to the other.

Clowns pretending they were women
Wore tight court shoes, and pulled outsize
Frocks down over plump balloon busts.
Dancing too close was unwise . . .
Bangs, and shock replaced their sheep's eyes.

Gillian C Fisher

Best Of British

I am an Antipodean
With British ancestors by birth
And what I see as best of British
Is their humorous mirth.

I've been to Land's End
Travelled to John o'Groats
Visited everything in-between
Especially castles with moats!

I've probably seen more of Britain
Than the average Brit around
And although I've toured the world
I reckon no humour like theirs is to be found.

I could mention many other things
That also do the British proud
Like their lovely countryside
Or the boisterous football crowd!

But the thing that really stands out
And this isn't just a rumour
Are all the friendly people
And that wonderful British humour!

Trudi Webber

BEST OF BRITISH

How proud I am to be British
In this green and pleasant land,
It stands for tolerance and justice,
With laws we can understand.

We have athletes and sportsmen,
All who are second to none
Our stately homes house nobility,
Whilst pleasure parks give fun.

But if it is the arts you seek
You don't have to look far
Our theatres and our studios
Are world famed for their charm.

But for me the best of British
Must surely be our Queen
Along with the Queen Mother
Who always appears serene.

They represent our country
So steadfastly and true
No wonder I want to shout out loud
Three cheers for the red, white and blue.

Winifred Lund

THE CAUSE

Why do they feel no grief
These men of clay?
They hear the cries of those in pain
And walk away
They do their job, we cry in vain
For their beliefs

They have no shame. They hide
Their dreadful deeds
Do they hear the pitiful moans
Of those bereaved?
How different are they from their own,
Those kids who died?

Do you not feel a touch of fear
You angry one
When alone and in your dreams
Their ghosts will come
Will you go mad or will you scream?
No one will hear.

They're not like us these men who laugh
At others' pain.
Their hearts belong to beast not man
Or they're insane.
We care not which, just let us plan
Their epitaph.

Arthur Denny

EARTH MAN
(The Report)

(a) We have been observing him. On the top liquid holes peer at you from a round piece that has strands of bright-coloured particles (called hair) coming out of it.

(b) There are four tentacles, two of which pick up objects while the other two lower tentacles are used to moved around. This they do by lifting up one tentacle, placing it forward then drawing up the other tentacle.

(c) They make covers for their lower tentacles by taking a special juice from some trees. Plants can be manipulated so that they can wear them This they call cloth.

(d) This creature has loose bags of flesh covered in skin which swing about as it moves. Its frame consists of a tubular sort of substance built up from calcium deposits.

(e) He makes strange liquids and places them in different shaped containers which he drinks usually when he mates.

(f) These creatures are made in shades of many colours but, they seem to hate each other if they do not use the same sort of noise when they (talk) this means moving the slit in the round piece rapidly.

(g) The thing that they do best is kill.

Jean Paisley

How To Create A Rose

First you need a seed:
Two people talking, finding out one another's needs.
The seed's now planted, but needs to be nurtured:
The secret glances, the warming smiles,
The accidental brush of each other's hands,
All these things together are needed to make
The heart of the flower, encased in a bud.
Eyes meeting, fusing together, embracing,
Exchanging warmth from one to another.
Caring and sharing, fun and laughter,
Sharing a private joke.
These are the things that create memories.
Each one of these creates the petals, overlapping one another.
The more memories, the stronger the rose.
Help push it open, for all to see.
The touch of the rose is the softness of your skin.
The smell of the rose is the scent you hold within.
The roots are the foundation, which grow down and down,
Making the rose safe and secure.
Which is how I feel, held in your arms.
As each petal falls, softly to the ground;
Don't mistake it for the end,
For each one represents another seed.
And that, my dear, is how love grows.

Teresa Connolly

The Millennium Year

The millennium year is approaching fast
By the march of old Father Time
The last countdown has started
And soon the bells will chime.
We eagerly await the millennium chimes
Only once in every thousand years
The Twenty-First Century is upon us
As we raise our glass with cheers.
We think back on all the happenings
And wonder what the future holds
Looking forward to better times
As this special year unfolds.
Let us try and make things better
And our resolutions keep
For life still goes on around us
The same old problems we have to meet
Our lives they span three score and ten
In the cycle of millennium time
Time is long in life's short cycle
If we hear the tithe bell chime
Let us now enjoy this special time
The countdown to a thousand more
Looking forward to the future
Old Father Time has seen it all before.

Frank Scott

A Pensive Ride

The sun is glistening on the frosted grass,
an air of spring about.
Clumps of snowdrops in the grass and crocuses
popping up here and there.
Purple bulb-shaped heads, some of yellow
and some with added colour stripes to the purple.
Rank outranked by rank, this special ride with no
time to tarry except for today
To read the plaques upon the wall.
In this peaceful resting place, rank is not the aim.
The simple crosses in the grass are that of human ash,
it shows man how crumbling is his rank.
Sun peeping through the bare black sculptured trees.
Primroses and daffodils growing merrily beneath,
Flowers of spring in abundance and plenty scattered
Human crosses, that will soon have the names carved
upon the wall, where all our pride is outranked.

Margaret Gleeson Spanos

To Myself

The age is looking like the year's time.
From spring to winter is not a long way.
From the first birthday when our eyes do shine
To the day of death, when our hairs are grey.

Now, I cannot turn around my whole life.
All the right thoughts came to me too late.
And when I see it's not far the dark night,
I cannot stop the life and say 'Wait!'

My age is equal to the time of autumn,
Ninety or more percent of life ran away.
I would like to prolong my years even in autumn.
I can't give an order to have them stay.

I try to adapt myself to this time.
I try to think it's good, it's nice, perfect.
When I see on my face a lot of lines,
My persuasion can't have a good effect.

But autumn is a wonderful time.
It's not too hot and still it's not too cold.
Vacations in autumn were my old flame.
The colour changes, around all is gold.

I have one way to adapt to my age:
To remember only good things from my life.
But sometimes my dreams are very strange.
All my bad life comes to the eyes at night.

Today I want to ask my God:
To give me gifts - some happy years.
The second that I need, my God:
To end my life without tears.

Anna Virkerman

OPENING
(For Steve)

Standing in the large sports hall,
music vibrating the floor.
Calling out to the others, unheard.
I close my eyes and listen.
The words from the song,
more meaningful somehow.
The locked door within me,
becomes unhinged and is taken away.
God is within me, and now;
is showing me the way.

Hannah Shooter